Jackie Robinson

by Jonatha A. Brown

Reading consultant: Susan Nations, M.Ed., author/literacy coach/consultant

WEEKLY WR READER
EARLY LEARNING LIBRARY

Please visit our web site at: www.earlyliteracy.cc
For a free color catalog describing Weekly Reader® Early Learning Library's list
of high-quality books, call 1-877-445-5824 (USA) or 1-800-387-3178 (Canada).
Weekly Reader® Early Learning Library's fax: (414) 336-0164.

Library of Congress Cataloging-in-Publication Data

Brown, Jonatha A.
    Jackie Robinson / by Jonatha A. Brown.
      p. cm. — (People to know)
    Includes bibliographical references and index.
    ISBN 0-8368-4311-8 (lib. bdg.)
    ISBN 0-8368-4318-5 (softcover)
    1. Robinson, Jackie, 1919–1972—Juvenile literature. 2. Baseball players—United States—Biography—
Juvenile literature. 3. African American baseball players—Biography—Juvenile literature. I. Raatma,
Lucia. Jackie Robinson. II. Title. III. People to know (Milwaukee, Wis.)
    GV865.R6B76 2004
    796.357'092—dc22
    [B]   2004044477

This edition first published in 2005 by
Weekly Reader® Early Learning Library
330 West Olive Street, Suite 100
Milwaukee, WI 53212 USA

Copyright © 2005 by Weekly Reader® Early Learning Library

Based on *Jackie Robinson* (Trailblazers of the Modern World series) by Lucia Raatma
Editor: JoAnn Early Macken
Designer: Scott M. Krall
Picture researcher: Diane Laska-Swanke

Photo credits: Cover, title, National Baseball Hall of Fame Library, Cooperstown, NY; pp. 4,
5, 13, 18 © Hulton Archive/Getty Images; pp. 7, 9, 10, 14, 15, 17, 20 © Bettmann/CORBIS;
p. 12 © National Baseball Hall of Fame Library/MLB Photos via Getty Images

Printed in the United States of America

1 2 3 4 5 6 7 8 9 08 07 06 05 04

Table of Contents

Words that appear in the glossary are printed in **boldface** type the first time they occur in the text.

Chapter 1: Childhood

Picking cotton is a nasty job. Mrs. Robinson did not want her children to have to pick cotton.

Jackie Robinson was born on January 31, 1919. His family lived in Cairo, Georgia. He had three brothers—Edgar, Frank, and Mack. He had a sister, too. Her name was Willa Mae. Jackie was the baby of the family.

When Jackie was only six months old, his father left home. Jackie's mother wanted to start a new life. She moved the family to Pasadena, California.

Mrs. Robinson found work as a maid. All day long, she worked for rich white people. At night, she had barely enough money to buy food for her children.

This is Jackie's family. Jackie is the boy in the hat.

In Pasadena, most of their neighbors were white. Some of them thought their white skin made them better than the Robinsons. Some did not want a black family to live on their street.

Many white children were mean to Jackie and his brothers and sisters. They called them ugly names. The Robinsons did their best to ignore the **insults**. They helped each other. And they stayed right there in the white neighborhood.

School Days

Jackie's mother worked long hours. Willa Mae took care of Jackie. When she went to school, he played in the sandbox there.

Finally, Jackie started school. He was not the best student, but he was a good **athlete**. Other students wanted him on their teams. They all tried to play better than Jackie did.

Jackie played football in high school.

Jackie's brothers were also good athletes. Mack even ran in the Olympics. Jackie looked up to his brothers.

In high school, Jackie played four sports. He played on the football, baseball, basketball, and track teams. He earned **letters** in every sport he played. He did the same thing in college. He was the first person at his college to earn letters in four sports.

Work and War

Jackie did not finish college. He left to look for a job. He worked for a group that helped young people in need. The group ran educational and athletic programs.

Jackie liked the work, but he did not keep his job for long. World War II had started. The United States needed his help.

Chapter 2: Army Life

In 1942, Jackie joined the army. He wanted to be an officer. He tried to join the officers' school, but that was not allowed. Only white men could go to that school.

Before long, the army changed its rules. They let a few black men become officers.

Joe Louis was a famous boxer. He helped black men get ahead in the army.

Jackie signed up for officers' school. He worked hard. Then the army made him an officer.

Jackie wanted to play sports in the army. He joined the football and baseball teams. After that, other teams would not play against his team. Those other teams had only white players. They did not want to play against a team with a black player.

Jackie was angry. He quit playing sports in the army. He said he would just be a soldier.

In movie theaters and other places, black people were not allowed to use the front door.

Even then, Jackie still faced problems because he was black. Once he was riding on an army bus. He was told to move to the back seat so white soldiers could sit in front. Jackie did not move. He said it was unfair. Jackie was called a troublemaker. He knew it was time to go. He left the army for good.

Unfair Laws

In those days, black people often had to sit in the back of a bus. Unfair laws in the South kept black people and white people apart. Black people could not eat in many places where white people did. They could not stay in the same hotels. They could not even go to the same schools. Black people did not have the same rights as white people.

Jackie needed a job. A soldier told him about an all-black baseball team. The team was looking for new players. That team was the Kansas City Monarchs. They played in an all-black baseball **league**. Jackie joined the team. He got to play ball and earn money at the same time.

This team played in an all-star game for an all-black league in 1948.

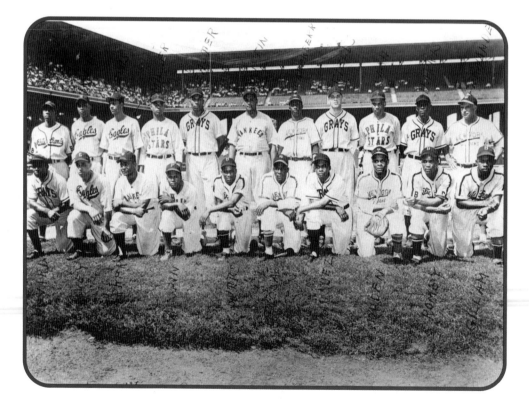

Chapter 3: "Play Ball!"

Jackie played well for the Monarchs. He played so well that a man named Branch Rickey noticed him. Mr. Rickey was the head of the **famous** Brooklyn Dodgers. The Dodgers were an all-white major league baseball team.

Branch Rickey thought that black and white players should play

Jackie played for the Kansas City Monarchs.

together. He did not care what color a man's skin was. He just wanted good players on his team.

Mr. Rickey asked Jackie to come to his office. They sat and talked. Mr. Rickey said it was time to make a change. He wanted black men to play on his white team. Mr. Rickey asked Jackie to join the Montreal Royals. The Royals were the Dodgers' minor league team for young white players. He said that as soon as Jackie was ready, he could join the Dodgers.

Jackie was thrilled. He was a little scared, too. He would be the only black player on the team. He would have to put up with insults and name-calling. But he knew he could succeed if he did not lose his temper.

Branch Rickey hired Jackie to play for the Brooklyn Dodgers.

Jackie hit a home run in his first game with the Montreal Royals.

In April 1946, Jackie played his first game for the Royals. He was nervous about the crowd. Soon it was his turn at bat. He hit the ball hard, but he was out.

The next time he came to bat, he swung hard again. That time, he hit a three-run home run! The crowd cheered for him. Jackie helped his team win that day. He was very proud.

Lonely at First

Being the first black player in a white league was not easy. At first, some of his teammates did not want him on the team. Some fans called him ugly names. They yelled at him to get off the field. Other players even tried to hurt him. But Jackie was careful to keep his temper. And many people were glad that the Royals had a great new player.

He played all summer. At the end of the season, the Royals won the Little World Series. In the last game, Jackie scored the winning run. Loyal fans cheered for him again. Jackie was a hero!

Chapter 4: Baseball Star

Leo Durocher was the Dodgers' manager. He was ready to have a black man on the team.

Jackie was ready to play for the Dodgers. But some of the Dodgers were not ready for him. A few said they would rather quit than play with a black man. Branch Rickey did not like that kind of talk.

He told those men they would not need to quit —
he would kick them off the team! When they heard
that, the men backed down.

Jackie joined the Dodgers in the spring of 1947.
He hoped to play well. He wanted to prove that he
belonged on that great team. But the first few games
were tough. He just could not seem to hit the ball.

Pee Wee Reese
was a shortstop
for the Dodgers.
He became
Jackie's friend.

Jackie had other problems, too. Most players were not friendly to him, and he felt lonely. People yelled insults at Jackie. They wanted to hurt his feelings. Their words made Jackie angry, but he did not let it show.

The Dodgers soon saw that Jackie had **courage**. He calmly faced people who screamed hateful things at him. He turned away from the insults. His teammates liked that. They began to make friends with him.

Better and Faster

Jackie began to play better. He hit the ball hard. He started getting on base. He started scoring runs. He was fast, too, and he could steal bases. By the end of the season, Jackie led the league in stolen bases. He was also named Rookie of the Year. That meant he was the best new ballplayer in the league.

Fans came to love Jackie. Here, Jackie greets fans in the Dominican Republic.

Jackie's success made him proud. It gave black people hope that they could succeed as he did.

Jackie played great baseball for many years. Then he was named to the Baseball Hall of Fame. His number 42 was **retired** from all of baseball.

Jackie Robinson proved that talent is more important than skin color. He led the way for other black athletes.

Life after Baseball

After he stopped playing baseball in 1957, Jackie Robinson kept working. He helped raise money for **civil rights** groups. He worked with Martin Luther King Jr. and other civil rights leaders. He helped open a bank that lent money to black businesses. He kept working for equal rights for black people.

Glossary

athlete — a person who is trained or skilled in a sport or game

civil rights — powers that are given to people of a country by law, such as the right to vote

courage — bravery

famous — well known

insults — rude, unkind words meant to hurt a person's feelings

league — a group of teams that play against each other

letters — awards given to athletes by schools

retired — taken out of service

For More Information

Books

Baseball's Greatest Hitters. Sydelle Kramer (Random House)

Jackie Robinson. Helen Frost (Chelsea House)

Jackie Robinson. Wil Mara (Children's Press)

Leagues Apart: The Men and Times of the Negro Baseball Leagues.
   Lawrence S. Ritter (HarperTrophy)

Teammates. Peter Golenbock (Gulliver Books)

Web Sites

Jackie Robinson and Other Baseball Highlights
lcweb2.loc.gov/ammem/jrhtml/jrhome.html
Historical documents from the Library of Congress

Sports Illustrated Kids: Jackie Robinson
www.sikids.com/news/blackhistory/jackierobinson.html
Brief biography and a collection of statistics

Index

About the Author

Jonatha A. Brown has written several books for children. She lives in Phoenix, Arizona, with her husband and two dogs. If you happen to come by when she isn't at home working on a book, she's probably out riding or visiting with one of her horses. She may be gone for quite a while, so you'd better come back later.